Let's talk about When someone Dies

MOLLY POTTER

ILLUSTRATED BY
SARAH JENNINGS

BLOOMSBURY EDUCATION

LONDON OXFORD NEW YORK NEW DELHI SYDNEY

For Claire – my quirky sister who wanted this book dedicated to her because she thinks we should all be talking about death more.

BLOOMSBURY EDUCATION
Bloomsbury Publishing Plc
50 Bedford Square, London, WC1B 3DP, UK
Bloomsbury Publishing Ireland Limited
29 Earlsfort Terrace, Dublin 2, D02 AY28, Ireland

BLOOMSBURY, BLOOMSBURY EDUCATION and the Diana logo are trademarks of Bloomsbury Publishing Plc
First published in Great Britain, 2018 by Bloomsbury Publishing Plc
This edition published in Great Britain, 2026 by Bloomsbury Publishing Plc
Text copyright © Molly Potter, 2018, 2026
Illustrations copyright © Sarah Jennings, 2018, 2026

A catalogue record for this book is available from the British Library

ISBN: HB: 978-1-47295-534-0; PB: 978-1-80199-435-4; ePDF: 978-1-47295-533-3; ePub: 978-1-47295-984-3

6 8 10 9 7 (hardback)
2 4 6 8 10 9 7 5 3 1 (paperback)

Printed and bound in China by RR Donnelley Asia Printing Company Ltd, Dongguan, Guangdong

To find out more about our authors and books visit www.bloomsbury.com and sign up for our newsletters

For product safety related questions contact productsafety@bloomsbury.com

Let's talk about When Someone Dies

MOLLY POTTER

ILLUSTRATED BY
SARAH JENNINGS

BLOOMSBURY EDUCATION
LONDON OXFORD NEW YORK NEW DELHI SYDNEY

Dear Reader,

Coping with the death of someone can be a very sad, stressful and confusing time, and grown ups don't always know how to explain this to you or how to answer all the questions you might have. Finding the right words to talk about death is difficult, and people struggle with what to say and how to manage all the emotions surrounding it. Because grown ups are worried about saying the wrong thing, they sometimes avoid talking about death altogether.

This book is all about death. It explains what death is, why people die, how people might react to someone dying and what happens after a person has died. It also looks at all the things you can do to help remember them.

You might be reading this book because someone you know has died or you might be reading it because you want to know more about death. Either way, you will find answers to lots of questions and also tips on how to cope with all the different feelings that might bubble up when someone you know dies.

It's good to know...

You might read this book on your own or an adult might be sharing it with you. Either way, if you end up confused about anything, ask an adult if they can help you understand.

Contents

What is death?

When we are alive, our hearts beat, we breathe, we eat, we drink, we feel cold and hot, we feel pain and we feel emotions. We can move, talk and think.

A dead person doesn't do any of these things.

When someone dies, their heart stops beating, they stop breathing and their brain shuts down. A dead person stops doing the things they did when they were alive.

When a person dies, they don't need their body anymore.
Dead people cannot go back to being the person
they were and they never come back to life.

It's important to know...

Some people get very ill before they die. This can mean they're in pain, no longer able to walk and are sometimes not aware of what's going on around them. When these people die, they're no longer in pain. Dead people often look really calm and peaceful.

Are there different words for death?

Because people feel so sad when someone dies, they don't like to just blurt out the word 'dead'. Instead, they use words they think sound gentler and less shocking or upsetting. When you're young, these words can seem confusing.

Some people say a person has 'passed away' or 'passed on' to mean the person has died. Other people might say that the dead person has 'gone to a better place' or 'gone to heaven'. Sometimes, when somebody dies, people say that they have 'lost' that person. These are all softer ways of saying that a person is dead.

Flo slipped away in her sleep.

Peggy is at rest now.

Raymond has gone to meet his maker.

Edith didn't make it.

It might surprise you to know...

There are also some funny or silly words that mean 'to die'. These include things like 'kicked the bucket', 'snuffed it', 'popped ones clogs' or 'pushing up the daisies'. These words tend not to be used by people who are still very upset about someone dying.

Why do people die?

Just like plants and animals, nobody lives forever. We will all die at some time in the future. For most people, this happens when they are old and have lived a long life. It's more unusual, but a small number of people die before they're old and this can be especially sad or seem unfair.

I want you to live for ever Grandad.

Some people die because they have a serious illness. Their bodies stop working and even though they try really hard, the doctors can't make them well again. Other people might die as the result of an accident that damages their body so it can't keep them alive anymore.

Nobody knows when they are going to die and most people live for a very long time.

It's important to know...

Sometimes death is described as 'going for a very long sleep that you never wake up from'. When people die, they look a bit like they are asleep because they are so still but sleep and death are very different. You are still alive when you sleep.

How will you **learn** that someone has died?

Sometimes we know that a person will die because they have been ill for some time and the doctors have said that they have a serious illness that will definitely make them die. When people die like this, everyone can be a bit more prepared for it. Knowing a person is going to die usually gives you a chance to say goodbye either in person or by sending a message. When the person dies, it's still very distressing but not a complete shock.

I love you Nana.

Other deaths are unexpected. This can be because a person has a sudden illness that kills them or they die in an accident. When a person dies like this, people learn about the death suddenly – often the grown ups and children in a family hear the news at the same time. This can make it very shocking for everyone.

When adults tell you that someone has died, they should be able to explain to you what happened and answer any questions you might have. Often, the adult who gives you the news will be really upset. If you see them crying, you could give them a hug. It's normal to cry when someone dies.

What might you feel when someone dies?

You might feel really, really sad for longer than you have done before.

You might feel angry – sometimes about the person dying and sometimes about other things.

You might feel worried about any changes that might happen because someone has died.

You might feel insecure and need lots of comfort and support.

You might feel alone.

confused
worried
angry

You might feel a mixture of feelings that are almost too hard to explain.

Sometimes the feelings might be really strong.

Sometimes you might feel normal – as if nothing has happened.

It's important to know...

The different feelings you might experience when someone dies can be almost impossible to explain – they might be painful and other times just make you feel numb. You might also be worried that if you ask adults questions, you will upset them. All of these ways of feeling are completely normal.

What might you **think** when someone dies?

You might wonder how your life will change.

You might keep wondering why people have to die.

You might really, really wish that the person could come back.

You might think about other people you care about dying (and this can make you worried).

You might think it was somehow your fault (it's not your fault).

You might find you can't concentrate because lots of different thoughts are swirling around in your head.

You might think a lot about the last time you saw the person who died and what you said to them.

You might wonder if your life will ever feel normal again.

It's important to know...

When someone dies, you might have lots of questions going round in your head. They might be simple like 'What do I tell my friends?' or more complicated like 'Where do dead people go?'. Adults will try to answer your questions, so don't be afraid to ask.

How might you **react** when someone dies?

You might want to be alone and hide away and not talk about anything.

We got a new kitten today.

You might have pretend conversations with the person who has died.

You might cry for a long time.

You might find it hard to sleep.

You might ask for lots of cuddles and want to hear kind words.

You might want to carry on as normal.

You might want to ask lots of questions about what happened.

You might want to talk about how much you miss the person who died.

It's important to know...

When someone dies, people behave in all sorts of different ways. You need to do whatever feels right for you but this might change from minute to minute, hour to hour or day to day.

What's a funeral?

Funerals can all be a bit different depending on the dead person's beliefs or religion, but they're always a special time for friends and family to come together to say goodbye to the person who died and to celebrate their life.

A funeral can happen outside, in a religious building or in a building specially built for the ceremony. There may be a coffin at the funeral which is a special box containing the dead person's body. At some funerals, the lid of the coffin is left open so that people can see the dead person and say goodbye.

There's usually music at funerals. It's often music that the dead person liked when they were alive. People also speak and share stories about the person who has died.

20

People often cry at funerals because they feel sad, but there can be laughter too as happy memories are shared, especially after the funeral when people come together to eat and drink.

People often wear black clothes to a funeral to show respect for the person who has died. Sometimes people prefer to wear bright clothes and make funerals colourful to make it more like a celebration of the person's life.

Some people send flowers to a funeral to show how much they loved the person or they might give money to a charity instead.

It's important to know...

It's good when children get to choose whether they want to go to a funeral or not. Those who go tend to think it's important to have had the chance to say goodbye.

What happens to a person's body after the funeral?

At a cremation...

At the end of the funeral, a curtain goes around the coffin and it's not seen again.

The body then goes into a special hot oven where it's turned into ashes.

The ashes are put in a container called an urn. This urn is given to the family of the dead person.

People can choose whether to keep or bury the ashes or they can scatter them at a place the dead person loved. This is another way of saying goodbye.

It might surprise you to know...

When a person first dies, their body is kept at the hospital in a special, very cold place called the morgue. Next, the body is taken to the funeral directors (the people who sort out the funeral) so it can be put in the coffin.

At a burial...

After the ceremony, the coffin is taken to a cemetery, graveyard or woodland.

The coffin is lowered into a special hole in the ground called a grave. This hole is then filled up with soil.

The person leading the ceremony will say some more words about the dead person.

At the end of the ceremony, people sometimes throw flowers or handfuls of soil onto the coffin as a final goodbye.

It's important to know...

The dead person no longer needs their body, they don't feel anything and don't think or do anything anymore.

What do people believe happens after death?

Nobody can prove what happens after death, but different people believe different things. Here are some of the beliefs:

Christians, Muslims and Jews believe that you can go to heaven and are reunited with God and then live forever in heaven.

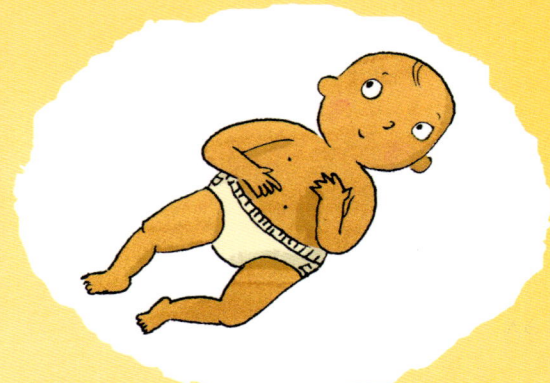

Buddhists, Sikhs and Hindus believe in reincarnation which means the person goes on to be born again into a different life.

Humanists believe that when you die that is simply the end.

Some people just accept that they have no idea what happens after a person dies.

Whatever you believe happens to a person after they've died, it's very normal to imagine they can still see you or for you to talk to them as if they're still alive. It can be comforting to imagine what the person might say at different times.

Although the person will never be seen again, their memory stays alive in the people who knew them.

It's important to know...

People often write RIP, which stands for Rest In Peace, when somebody has died. It comes from the olden days when nearly everyone believed in heaven or an afterlife and liked to think the person they loved had gone to a peaceful place after they died.

What happens in the weeks and months after someone has died?

Grown ups often say that time heals. This means that, as the days, weeks and eventually years go by, the strong emotions we felt when someone first died become less strong. This doesn't mean we love the person who died any less, it just means we have managed most of the painful feelings and can start to remember the person with more positive and happy feelings.

You may miss the dead person a lot and wish they could be with you again. This can still bring up strong emotions, but this is perfectly normal. It's important to find ways to remember the person who died. The next page gives you some suggestions about how you can do this.

Dad would have loved today. I miss him.

It's important to know...

After someone dies, your life carries on and this is how the person who died would have wanted it to be. They would want you to be happy and enjoy your life.

To remember a person who has died, you could...

Light a candle every year on their birthday.

Create a special place in your garden in memory of the person. Plant a tree or some flowers there.

Make a book about the person. Include their life story, describe their personality, list some of their favourite things and things you remember them saying.

She helped me when

Ask people to write down their best memory of the person and make a poster of these. (You could include a photo of them.)

Make a collection of photos, letters and possessions of the person who died and put them in a special memory box.

On special days, write a letter to the person who died.

Visit the grave or favourite place of the person who died and take a card or some flowers.

Keep sharing memories of the person who died with the people who also knew them.

Guidance for parents and carers

Death is an inevitable part of our everyday lives and yet it's still generally a taboo subject because it creates uncomfortable or painful feelings. Discussing death with children can be even more taboo. Attempts to protect children in this way mean information is often withheld from them. This is actually the opposite of what is best for them.

This book has been written with all children in mind – those who have been bereaved and those who have not. It can be shared with the latter group to inform them about death and thus equip them for bereavement when it happens, but it can also be used with children who have been recently bereaved. The advice on the following pages will help you get the most out of sharing this book with a child.

Some tips on talking to a child about death

- Their capacity for understanding death will depend on the age and development stage of the child. A two-year-old's grieving will be different from a six-year-old's.

- Be as open and honest as you can about what has happened. It's better if children aren't 'protected' as they'll pick up that something is wrong but be confused by the lack of information.

- Explain death in simple terms using straightforward language. Use the word 'died' instead of euphemisms as these can confuse children. Some children might be muddled about what death actually means. Use the description in this book or any other experiences of death the child might have encountered (e.g. death of a pet) to help explain what death means. You need to help the child understand that death is final and the person will not be coming back.

- Try not to anticipate their reaction. Children will react in a variety of ways – including carrying on as normal. There isn't a 'right' way to react. Explain to the child that when someone dies, they might experience lots of different feelings and that you're there to share those feelings with them.

- Don't hide your own sadness. Explain that you are crying because you feel really sad because you loved the person a lot.

- Let the child ask as many questions as they want. If you're unable to answer their questions because you're upset, reassure the child and tell them that you'll tell them everything in due course.

- Explain any practical changes that might happen as a result of the death. Outline all the routines that will stay the same for the child so they feel reassured and comforted.

- Make it very clear that nobody could have done anything to stop the death and that it was nobody's fault as some children may blame themselves.

Answering children's questions

Children might surprise you with what they ask. Their questions can range from asking about practicalities to those that could be seen as a macabre interest in the details of death. Attempt to answer their questions as openly and honestly as you can and if you don't know the answer – say so. Try hard not to fabricate softer answers as you may well lose their trust. Also be aware that they might bombard you with questions and then suddenly seem like they've had enough, only to continue the next day with more.

Attending a funeral

It's best to give the child the choice of whether to go a funeral or not. It's as much an opportunity for them to say goodbye as it is for everyone else. They don't need to be 'protected' from the ceremony. Children that attend funerals generally don't say that they regretted it.

Prior to the funeral, explain to the child exactly what will happen. If possible, with younger children, arrange for a trusted adult to be available should the child wish to leave at any point. If a child cannot attend for any reason, let them know what happened, answer any questions they have about the ceremony, and let them have their own ceremony to say goodbye if they want to.

The grieving process

Reactions to death are many and varied. However, there are generally recognised stages that go from shock, denial and the accompanying numbness to the more active grieving involving a cocktail of emotions including depression, despair, anger, guilt, and finally acceptance. No one person experiences grief in a truly linear way. Grieving is different for every individual and children may be even less predictable in how they respond to death. If your child is very young, they might not grasp the finality of death until after the age of five. Some reactions to death from young children include:

- Becoming more needy of hugs and reassurance;

- Having nightmares and difficulty sleeping;

- Struggling to express how they are feeling and becoming withdrawn;

- Feeling guilty because they somehow think they were responsible for the death because they were cross with the person, for example;

- Reverting to behaviours they exhibited when they were younger;

- Becoming aggressive;

- Getting ill more often;

- Finding it difficult to concentrate;

- Engaging in obsessive behaviours.

Positive grieving

Grieving is a process that takes time. It's about accepting the loss and finding ways of moving on in life while still being able to remember the person and what they meant to you. To do this, a child needs to be able to express and share any strong emotions they have and be able to talk openly about the person who died when they want to. Further things that help with grieving include:

Continuing to answer any questions they have about what happened and what will happen:

Reassuring them that they are still cared for, safe and loved and that their world won't fall apart completely:

Being able to give and receive comfort and support

yourself. A well-supported parent will be better equipped to support their child:

Sticking to the same routine as much as possible:

Having open discussions about what they are finding difficult now and at different stages throughout the grieving process.

Remember...

An important part of the grieving process is to not only talk openly about feelings but also about the person who has died. Regular family rituals can help with this. Making collections of memories, possessions and photos of the dead person stored in a box that a child can access at any time is also a good idea.